Teaching Children Simple Ways to Pray

by Kass Perry Dotterweich

*A*s parents, we want the best for our children. So it is only natural that we want to impart to them the riches of praying.

For prayer is the repository of the intimacy we share with God, who rests **within us and** who invites us into a union beyond human comprehension. Through prayer we come to know and respond to the unconditional—and ultimately unfathomable—love of God.

The fact that we are even remotely aware of the value of prayer, are stirred to prayer, and want to instill in our children some simple practices of prayer is itself prayer!

Enriching your prayer life

There are as many ways to teach children simple ways to pray as there are children to be taught. Be creative, depending on your family makeup and specific circumstances. Be alert for that special moment pregnant with God's invitation to be in communion.

As you teach your child to pray, keep in mind certain theological basics. You do not want to convey that God is a distant God. Rather, build in your child an awareness of a near-at-hand God, God within.

Do not give your child a "jolly-Santa-in-the-sky" image of God, a God who grants wishes in some magical manner. When your child prays for something specific and doesn't "get it," he or she begins to distrust this kind of God.

Finally, do not imply that we have to pray to get to heaven. You cannot foster a healthy relationship with God with a payoff mentality.

◆ *Pray familiar prayers.* The prayers of our childhood are wellsprings of meaning and tradition. When you tuck your child into bed for the first time without a night-light, help him or her memorize a line from the 23rd Psalm: "Even though I walk in the dark valley I fear no evil; for you are at my side...."

The next night, repeat the line again. Eventually, the prayer becomes routine. Both of you may even forget the original experience of fear.

In helping your youngster memorize prayers, take short sections at a time and explain them. Phrases like "...from thy bounty..." and "...forgive us our trespasses..." will be foreign to children. Ex-

Creating your own prayer experience

Praying the Quiet

Ask your child to recall a conversation with a friend. Remind him or her how important it was to listen and to be heard. Link this to prayer: God has much wisdom to convey to us—and, like talking with a friend, hearing is difficult if there's noise.

Begin family meals with a full minute of quiet. Turn off the television and invite your child to listen with expectation to the quiet. Draw the child's attention to the deep, awesome quiet of a night sky. Have your child imagine that his or her heart is a small room in the center of his or her body. Tell your child to go into that little room, sit quietly, and listen for the soft whisper of God's love.

"One of the best times to get the kids in touch with quiet," one mother shares, "is when they awaken in the middle of the night for some reason. After we've taken care of a trip to the bathroom, a drink of water, or reassurance after a bad dream, I tell them to listen to the quiet of the house. I remind them that God likes to use those quiet times to talk to us in special ways."

plain these phrases in terms your youngster will understand. Memorization is made easier and the tendency to pray is reinforced if the child comprehends the meaning behind the words.

*"**D**ear God, when is the best time I can talk with you? I know you are always listening, but when will you be listening especially hard in Ann Arbor, Michigan?"*
—"Allen," in *The Children's God* by David Heller

Establish a routine time for these prayers. All good habits have more staying power if they fit into a familiar routine: before and after meals, before bed, before catching the school bus.

◆ *Pray memories.* Children of all ages love to remember. They like to think about their last birthday, last Christmas, when Cousin Alice stayed overnight, the first time they got to drive the car. Use these times of musing to call your child into prayer.

"Ah, yes, your last birthday. God has blessed us with so much laughter and happiness because you're in our lives."

"Jesus helped us celebrate last Christmas in a special way by putting joy in our hearts even though we didn't have much money for presents."

"The last time Alice spent the night with us, she

was so afraid. Let's pray that she feels God's arms around her so she won't be afraid this time."

"From the minute you picked up the keys off the counter and headed for the driveway, I prayed for your good judgment and my patience."

Praying memories can help a child accept the death of a loved one as well. Help your child recall special characteristics and events about that person; praise God for the life that person—now so greatly missed—shared with others.

Children of all ages can experience—if not understand—how remembering sanctifies life itself, which is what prayer is all about. Turn memories into prayers of thanksgiving and praise.

◆ *Pray emotions.* Childhood emotions are poignant: fear, happiness, confusion, anticipation, disappointment. Prayer is a way children learn to befriend their emotions.

When a strong feeling erupts, ask your child to draw it on a sheet of paper. Anger, for example, might be expressed by dark jagged slashes; hope, by sweeping rainbow-type arches. Assure your child that the drawing is a prayer, a personal prayer, a special conversation between him or her and God; no

Your child should understand that prayer is an important gift from God. The more we use it the more beautiful it becomes. Even when we are unsure how to pray and what to say, words can flow from our hearts....Prayers are not necessarily a series of words repeated over and over again from memory. Prayer is a heart attitude and the expressing of our innermost self to God.

—Frances Loftiss Carroll
How to Talk With Your
Children About God

one else will see the drawing.

When the drawing is finished, have the child put it in a special place: inside the front cover of the family Bible, behind a crucifix in the dining room, or on the floor in the back of his or her closet—wherever the child is comfortable leaving it. Tell the child that placing the drawing in a special place is like placing the emotion in God's lap.

Believe it or not, teenagers can get into this form of prayer. A slight modification (one with a little more drama) is to ignite the paper from a ritual candle or toss it into a campfire. This appeals to the older children's need for action (ritual), and it helps make tangible that which is abstract (symbolism).

◆ *Pray the moment.* Psalm 139 addresses a God who nurtures and sustains our very existence. Every second of the day is made possible by God's providential grace. Drawing a child's attention to this fact is an ever-present opportunity.

Pray the sunrise, the refreshing feeling of a morning shower, the feel of clean underwear, the traffic, the fun at recess, the smelly feet as the tennis shoes are kicked off.

What? Pray smelly feet? Indeed. Explain to your child that God created everything—*everything*—about our bodies.

Take the child's hand and place it on your chest. Let him or her feel the rhythm of your heartbeat and explain: "God keeps our hearts beating." And, conversely, when a heart stops beating, God is there to strengthen the broken hearts that remain.

One father asks his children to "pray the siren." When they hear the blare of emergency vehicles, they place in God's special care all the people involved: victims, families, emergency and medical personnel.

Lifting your heart to God

When it comes right down to it, words, positions, times of day, activity, and even disposition are irrelevant to praying. Simply invite your child to speak his or her thoughts and emotions to God.

St. Therese of Lisieux said about prayer, "I do as a child would who cannot read—I just say what I want to say to God, quite simply, and he never fails to understand."

What a wonderful directive for teaching children to pray! ◆

Exploring Further

Books: *Prayer and Our Children* by Mary Terese Donze, A.S.C., Notre Dame, Indiana, Ave Maria, 1987. *God and You: Prayer as a Personal Relationship* by William A. Barry, Mahwah, New Jersey, Paulist, 1987. *The Family Book of Prayer* by Tony Castle, Collegeville, Minnesota, Liturgical Press, 1991. *In My Heart Room* (Books I and II) by Mary Terese Donze, A.S.C., Liguori, Missouri, Liguori Publications, 1982, 1990.

Kass Perry Dotterweich is the mother of six children and a book editor for Liguori Publications.

PrayerNotes™
from Abbey Press

Visit our website at: www.prayernotes.com.

Call us toll free: 1-800-325-2511

Printed on recycled paper.

25009